# The Incom

CW01645798

W. J. McDOWELL

*Minister of*
*The Evangelical Presbyterian Church*
*Belfast, Northern Ireland*

THE BANNER OF TRUTH TRUST

THE BANNER OF TRUTH TRUST
3 Murrayfield Road, Edinburgh EH12 6EL
P.O Box 621, Carlisle, Pennsylvania 17013, USA

★

© The Banner of Truth Trust 1988

ISBN 0 85151 543 6

★

Typeset at The Spartan Press Ltd,
Lymington, Hants
Printed in Great Britain by
Macdonald Printers Ltd, Loanhead.

# Introduction

What David said about Goliath's sword can be applied to the Bible: 'There is none like it'. It is the Incomparable Book.

The Bible societies are continually appealing for money to enable them to translate and circulate the Holy Scriptures. Millions of copies of the whole Bible are in circulation in many parts of the world, and many thousands of other books have been published to explain it, to criticize it, or to defend it. This extraordinary Book begins its story before the dawn of history and ends it after the conclusion of all possible human records.

Its chief subject is God. His Names, his words, and his deeds are found on nearly every page. Man by searching cannot find out God. Such knowledge is too lofty for him to acquire by his own efforts. It has been well said that man could not have written such a book if he would, and that he would not if he could.

Nowhere in the whole range of literature is so much stupendous truth conveyed in such simple language, in so small a compass.

Dr B. B. Warfield points out that this remarkable volume consists of 'no less than sixty-six separate books' that 'come from the hands of at least thirty distinct writers, scattered over a period of some fifteen hundred years . . . and a most striking unity is found to pervade the whole . . . Unless we are prepared to allow a man some fifteen hundred years of conscious existence and intellectual supervision of the work, we are shut up here to the admission of a superhuman origin for this book'.[1]

[1] *Revelation and Inspiration*, Oxford University Press, 1927, pp. 436–7.

## *It Speaks With Authority*

A spirit of authority and certainty pervades the Bible. Suppositions, suggestions and conjectures are absent from its pages. We read continually: 'Thus saith the Lord'. Dr S. H. Kellogg remarks concerning the Book of Leviticus: 'Perhaps no book in the Bible presents to the ordinary reader so many and peculiar difficulties as the book of Leviticus', yet 'no less than fifty-six times' do we meet with expressions like 'The Lord called unto Moses', 'The Lord spake unto Moses'.[1] That means that Leviticus contains 56 statements from the Lord, or else 56 false affirmations of such statements. The very thought is blasphemous.

*Its promises are emphatic.* Take one example: 'He hath said, I will never leave thee, nor forsake thee' (Heb. 13:5). 'This promise contains the sum and substance of all the promises' is the remark in Matthew Henry's Commentary, adding an observation based on the original Greek text: 'Here are no less than five negatives heaped together to confirm the promise: the true believer shall have the gracious presence of God with him in life, at death and for ever'. It is well paraphrased in the words:

> The soul that on Jesus has leaned for repose
> I will not, I will not desert to its foes;
> That soul, though all hell should endeavour to shake,
> I'll never, no, never, no never forsake!

*Its commandments are decisive.* They are not just words of advice. Some things are clearly commanded. Others are plainly forbidden. Our conduct is not to be governed by popular opinion, nor by personal preferences. Writing on the Ten Commandments Bishop Hopkins declares: 'The words are few . . . but the sense and matter contained in them is

[1] *The Book of Leviticus*, Hodder & Stoughton, 1911, p. 5.

vast and infinite. The rest of Scripture is but a commentary upon them: either exhorting us to obedience by arguments, or alluring us to it by promises, or frighting us from transgressing by threatenings; or exciting us to the one, and restraining us from the other, by examples recorded in the historical part of it'.[1]

*Its threatenings are awesome.* We read: 'Cursed is everyone that continueth not in all things which are written in the book of the law to do them' (Gal. 3:10). 'Though hand join in hand, the wicked shall not be unpunished' (Prov. 11:21). The Bible's teaching on future, eternal punishment caused C. H. Spurgeon to pray: 'Lord, by thy good spirit, keep me ever in mind of that great day of days, which will make eternity bright with immeasurable bliss, or dark with unutterable woe! May I look at everything in the blaze of light which surrounds thy judgment seat!'[2]

## *Its Words are from God*

The Holy Scriptures claim that they have come to us directly from the Lord. One of the Apostles declares: 'Holy men of God spake as they were moved by the Holy Ghost' (2 Pet. 1:21). Dr Lloyd-Jones' comment is: 'The great claim that is made is this, that these men were taken hold of by the Holy Spirit. The Holy Spirit came upon them and took hold of them and gave them a message, carried them along, drove them along as they wrote and put it down on record'.

The same writer points out that in the account of Paul's shipwreck in Acts 27:17 we are told that the ship was 'driven' – 'that is', he says 'the very same word' used in 2 Peter 1:21.[3]

[1] *The Ten Commandments*, Hopkins' Works, Henry G. Bohn, 1846, p. 4.
[2] *The Gospel of the Kingdom*, Passmore & Alabaster, 1893, p. 139.
[3] *Truth Unchanged, Unchanging*, The Bible League, 1984, p. 158.

But some will object, 'But that means mechanical dictation, which would curb the personal freedom of the writers'. In answer it may be affirmed that a comparison of the different parts of the Bible with each other will not allow for any idea of mechanical dictation. R. M. McCheyne expresses this in his well-known hymn:

> I oft read with pleasure, to soothe or engage,
> Isaiah's wild measure and John's simple page.

'What a wonderful variety there is in the Bible', remarks Dr Machen. 'There is the rough simplicity of Mark, the unconscious, yet splendid eloquence of Paul, the conscious literary art of the author of the Epistle to the Hebrews, the matchless beauty of the Old Testament narratives, the high poetry of the Prophets and the Psalms. How much we should lose, to be sure, if the Bible were written all in one style!' Machen goes on to say: 'This doctrine of inspiration is certainly a great paradox. It holds that these men were free, and yet that every word that they wrote was absolutely determined by the Spirit of God. How is that possible? How could God determine the very words that these men wrote and yet not deal with them as mere machines? I will tell you how God could do that. He could do it simply because God is God'.[1]

Another passage that directs our attention to the Divine origin of the Scriptures is 2 Timothy 3:16–17: 'All Scripture is given by inspiration of God . . . '. No doubt there are some wonderful passages in the Bible that 'inspire' us to be better Christians, but that is not the Apostle's meaning in these verses. E. J. Young declares that 'the Scriptures . . . are writings which came into being because they were breathed out by God himself. And that is something quite different from what is commonly suggested by the word "inspiration"'. The same writer also remarks: 'First and foremost in our study of the Scriptural doctrine of inspiration we must vigorously

[1] *The Christian Faith in the Modern World*, 61. Hodder & Stoughton, 1936, pp. 59, 61.

assert the fact that Scripture regards itself as God-breathed'.[1]

Referring to 2 Timothy 3:16 and 2 Peter 1:21, Professor John Murray says: 'These two texts have closer relationship to one another than we might be disposed to think. For in the usage of Scripture the Word of God, the breath of God, and the Spirit of God are closely related. And when Paul says "all Scripture is God-breathed", he is saying nothing less than that all Scripture is God's speech, God's voice invested with all the authority and power belonging to his utterance. Peter explains how what is given through the agency of men can be God's speech – "as borne by the Holy Spirit men spoke from God"'.[2]

The words of the Bible are God's words. Without being irreverent we might ask: 'If God did not communicate his messages to the writers of the Bible in words how did he communicate them?' Caught up into Paradise Paul heard words that he was not permitted to tell (2 Cor. 12:4). Nevertheless the communication was in 'words'. As Dr George Smeaton expresses it: 'We cannot have accurate ideas without precise words, nay, we cannot think without words.'[3]

Not every word found in the Holy Book was spoken by God. Good men speak, bad men speak, the devil speaks, and the record of what they say is controlled by God, so that the account is given correctly. The Psalmist exclaims, 'The fool hath said in his heart, there is no God' (Psa. 14:1). It is not true that there is no God, but it is true that the fool says so in his heart. The saying is false, but the record of it is true.

The Bible chronicles events that are contrary to the principles it declares. Abraham and Isaac lied. David committed adultery and murder. Jeroboam set up idols. Ananias and Sapphira tried to deceive God. Such deeds are contrary to the Ten Commandments. They are not recorded

[1] *Thy Word is Truth*, Banner of Truth Trust, 1963, pp. 22, 23.
[2] *Collected Writings*, Vol. 1, Banner of Truth Trust, 1976, pp. 12, 13.
[3] *The Doctrine of the Holy Spirit* T & T Clark, 1889, p. 171, footnote.

for our imitation, but as warnings against doing such things, and to show us their evil consequences.

When Peter and Paul wrote the words we have quoted about the inspiration of the Scriptures, the New Testament as we now have it was not in circulation among the churches. Does divine direct verbal inspiration apply only to the Old Testament? The answer to that question can be given in the words of Johannes G. Vos: 'The two Testaments are organically interrelated, each being incomplete and unintelligible without the other'.[1] Dr Vos's statement is strengthened when we read in Angus and Green's *Bible Handbook* that the number of quotations from the Old Testament in the New Testament has been 'reckoned to amount to 263; references less direct being in number 376, or together, 639'.[2]

Peter puts Paul's writings on the same level as other parts of the Bible when he says that Paul has written some things hard to understand 'which they that are unlearned and unstable wrest as they do also the other scriptures, unto their own destruction' (2 Pet. 3:16). The same Apostle speaks of the words 'which were spoken before by the holy prophets', and of 'the commandment of us the apostles' as of equal authority.

In 1 Timothy 5:18 Paul declares: 'The Scripture saith, Thou shalt not muzzle the ox that treadeth out the corn. And, the labourer is worthy of his reward'. The first sentence is a quotation from Deuteronomy 25:4, and the second is found in Luke 10:7. Both are spoken of as 'the Scripture'.

It is evident that the Bible itself is not responsible for the attitude of those who pit the Old Testament against the New Testament. In time past God spoke by the prophets. In these last days He has spoken by his Son (Heb. 1:1–2). The words of the Old Testament and the words of the New Testament are equally the words of God.

If we inquire, How did God cause the writers of the Bible to write his words? we must reply, We do not know. To quote the

[1] *The Encyclopaedia of Christianity*, Vol. 1 1964, p. 655.
[2] *The Bible Handbook*, Religious Tract Society, 1907, p. 249.

words of E. J. Young: 'God has not seen fit to reveal to us the mode by which he communicated his word to his servants, placing that word in their mouths and "carrying" them until the Word was accurately committed to writing. We have come, in other words, into an area of mystery. There is much about this precious Scriptural doctrine which God has not revealed. The Scripture is silent as to the mode which God employed to preserve his word from error. In this as in so many doctrines of the Bible there is mystery'.[1]

Dr John Macleod expressed the same idea when he said: 'We, who cannot tell how soul and body co-exist and go to make up our full person, are overstepping the bounds of our province when we speculate as to how God is working in bringing such a product as Holy Writ into being'.[2]

Concerning the work of Creation we are told God 'spake, and it was done'. So concerning the production of his word we could say, 'He spoke, and it was written'.

## *It is Dependable in Translation*

Most of us read the Bible in a translation. Some Christian people may be disturbed by the publication of new versions of the Bible because they have been familiar with the Authorized Version for many years. A look at the title page of that version shows that when it was first published in 1611 there had been 'former translations'. They were Tyndale, 1525–1537; the Great Bible, 1539; the Geneva Bible, 1560; Bishop's Bible, 1568.

In the original preface of the AV the translators state: 'Translation it is that openeth the window to let in the light; that breaketh the shell that we may eat the kernel; that

[1] *Thy Word is Truth*, Banner of Truth Trust, 1963, pp. 70, 71.
[2] *The Evangelical Quarterly*, Vol. 7, No. 1.

putteth aside the curtain that we may look into the most holy place; that removeth the cover of the well that we may come by the water, even as Jacob rolled away the stone from the mouth of the well by which the flocks of Laban were watered. Indeed, without translation into the vulgar tongue the unlearned are but like children at Jacob's well (which was deep) without a bucket or something to draw with'.

Later on in the same Preface we are told: 'We affirm and avow, that the very meanest translation of the Bible in English . . . containeth the Word of God, nay, is the Word of God. As the King's speech which he uttered in Parliament, being translated into French, Dutch, Italian, and Latin, is still the King's speech, though it be not interpreted by every translator with the like grace, nor peradventure so fitly for phrase, nor so expressly for sense, everywhere . . . [There is] no cause therefore why the Word translated should be denied to be the Word, or forbidden to be current, notwithstanding that some imperfections and blemishes may be noted in the setting forth of it'.[1]

Does the increasing number of translations mean that the subject of direct verbal inspiration of the original autographs is only of historical interest? Has the authority of Holy Scripture been squeezed out by much copying and many translations? Sir Robert Anderson used the following illustration to meet that difficulty: 'When Xerxes issued his great proclamation in favour of the Jews, it was sent, we are told, to each of the hundred and twenty-seven provinces of the Empire, from India to Ethiopia, "and unto every people after their language". Could any of the nations have pleaded a wrong or a disability because the royal commands reached them only in their own dialect or tongue? Was not this altogether an advantage and a benefit? We may be sure that the great king would have made short work of such a grievance, and of those who urged it. He would have judged,

[1]The Original Preface to the Authorized Version, Trinitarian Bible Society, 1911, pp. 13, 23.

and rightly judged, that the objection was merely an excuse for disaffection or disobedience'.[1]

Writing in 1936 Dr Machen said: 'Very wonderfully and very graciously, according to our view of the Bible, has God provided for the preservation, from generation to generation, of his holy Word. What is the result? The result is that you can take down your Authorized Version from the shelf, the version hallowed, for many of you, by many precious associations, and be very sure that it will give you good information about that which stood in the autographs of the Word of God'.[2]

## *It is Infallible and Inerrant*

If we agree that the Holy Bible comes to us directly from God then we must accept that it is true and correct in all its statements. But there are some who will grant that Holy Writ is reliable and authoritative in all matters of faith and conduct, but who also think that its veracity can be challenged when it deals with such subjects as history and science. They hold that it is a mixture of divine truth and human error. But who will decide what parts of the Bible are reliable, and what parts are unreliable? The only possible answer is: We ourselves will so decide, that is, fallible men will judge between the infallible and the fallible.

If God created the universe then it is surely common sense that he will know all about its component parts. Will he allow the writers of his word to make scientific blunders? Some may ask, Why did Moses state that the sun rose upon Jacob as he passed over Penuel (Gen. 32:31)? Surely he must have thought that the sun moved around the earth. Is not this a

[1] *The Bible and Modern Criticism*, p. 95.
[2] *The Christian Faith in the Modern World*, p. 50.

mistake? But how then should Moses have stated the matter? Should he have said: 'The movement of the earth on its axis resulted in the sun appearing as Jacob passed over Penuel'? No one ever talks like that. Even the current issue of *Whitaker's Almanac* uses the expressions of 'sunrise' and 'sunset'. 'If Scripture uses the language of common usage and experience or observation', says Professor John Murray, 'we are not to accuse it of error because it does not use the language of a particular science, language which few could understand and which becomes obsolete with the passing phases of scientific advancement. The Scripture does not make itself ridiculous by conforming to what pedants might require'.[1]

Seeing that God governs the world, removing kings, and setting up kings (Dan. 2:21), we can be sure that he knows the names of all those who have ruled, and the countries they have governed, and the dates of their reigns. Is it likely that the absolute Controller of history would permit his penmen to make historical blunders?

There have been those who have presumed to question the historical accuracy of the Scriptures. E. J. Young quotes R. H. Charles (1855–1931) as saying: 'This chapter (Daniel 5) is notable for its historical inconsistencies'. Young's comment on this statement is: 'Such a sweeping statement, however, will not stand the test of close investigation. We prefer to write, "This chapter is notable for its remarkable accuracies."'[2] In Halley's *Bible Handbook* there is an archaeological note on Daniel 5:

'Until 1853 no mention of Belshazzar was found in Babylonian records: and Nabonidas, 555–538 B.C. was known to have been the last king of Babylon. To the critics this was one of the evidences that the book of Daniel was not historical. But in 1853 an inscription was found in a corner stone of a temple built by Nabonidas, in Ur to a god, which read: "May I, Nabonidas, king of Babylon, not sin against

[1]*Collected Writings*, Vol. 1, Banner of Truth Trust, 1976, pp. 14–15.
[2]*Daniel*, Banner of Truth Trust, 1978, p. 115.

thee. And may reverence for thee dwell in the heart of Belshazzar, my first-born, favourite son".

'From other inscriptions it has been learned that Nabonidas, much of the time, was in retirement outside of Babylon, and that Belshazzar was in control of the army and the government, co-regent with his father, and that it was he who surrendered to Cyrus. This explains how Daniel could be "third ruler" in the kingdom (Dan. 5:29). "Thy father Nebuchadnezzar" (verse 11) means, not actual father, but royal ancestor on the throne.'[1]

If the Bible contained errors concerning things that can be tested like geography and history we could not depend upon its statements about the unseen and eternal world. The God who 'cannot lie' would not allow the writers of his Book to record untruths. Our Lord Jesus, who is 'the truth' said to his Father 'Thy word is truth'.

The starry firmament on high,
And all the glories of the sky,
Yet shine not to thy praise, O Lord,
So brightly as thy written word.

Almighty Lord, the sun shall fail,
The moon forget her nightly tale,
And deepest silence hush on high,
The radiant chorus of the sky;

But, fixed for everlasting years,
Unmoved, amid the wreck of spheres,
Thy word shall shine in cloudless day,
When heaven and earth have passed away.[2]

[1]Halley's *Bible Handbook*, 1950, p. 308.
[2]*The Word of God and the Reformed Faith*, Baker's Book Store, 1943, p. 79.

## *It is Self-Authenticating*

Some may wish for external proofs that the Holy Scriptures are completely reliable, infallibly true, and possess divine authority. Christians accept the Bible's teaching on God, sin, salvation, the unseen world, etc. In the same way we must accept its teaching about itself. In John Murray's words: 'The doctrine of the infallibility of Scripture is derived from the witness of Scripture'. He also declares that it is impossible 'to produce by evidence extraneous to the Scripture the faith which has as its object the Scripture itself. The Reformers were aware of the fallacy attaching to argumentation on the basis of extrinsic evidence, and so they laid down the principle that Scripture is autopistic, that is, self-authenticating, and this means that the evidence validating the faith of Scripture as the word of God is the Scripture itself. This is to say that it contains within itself the evidence of its divine origin, character, and authority'.[1]

Let us hear, briefly, the testimony of the Lord Jesus, who spoke as never man spoke and who declared: 'All power [authority] is given unto me in heaven and in earth'. To quote R. B. Kuiper: 'Did not Jesus himself tell us that the Bible is infallible? He asserted, "The Scripture cannot be broken" and affirmed, "Thy word is truth" (John 10:35, 17:17). He declared, "Think not that I am come to destroy the law or the prophets: I am not come to destroy, but to fulfil. For verily I say unto you, Till heaven and earth pass, one jot or one tittle shall in no wise pass from the law, till all be fulfilled" (Matt. 5:17–18). If the written word is not infallible, the personal Word is a liar. In short, nothing could be clearer than that the

[1] *Collected Writings*, Banner of Truth Trust, 1976, Vol. 1. p. 13; Vol. 2, 1977, p. 241.

infallibility of the Bible and the infallibility of the Christ stand or fall together. He who denies the former rejects the latter'.[1]

There is also the evidence that cannot be logically demonstrated but is known only by believers in Christ, namely, the testimony of the Holy Spirit of God to the truth of his own word. Unbelievers may be silenced by other evidences, but they will not be convinced in their hearts apart from the testimony of the Spirit. John Calvin states this in his *Institutes*: 'The testimony of the Spirit is superior to all reason. For as God alone is a sufficient witness of himself in his own word, so also the word will never gain credit in the hearts of men till it be confirmed by the internal testimony of the Spirit. It is necessary, therefore, that the same Spirit, who spoke by the mouths of the prophets, should penetrate into our hearts to convince us that they faithfully delivered the oracles which were divinely intrusted to them . . . Let it be considered, then, as an undeniable truth, that they who have been inwardly taught by the Spirit, feel an entire acquiescence in the Scripture, and that it is self-authenticated, carrying with it its own evidence, and ought not to be made the subject of demonstration and arguments from reason; but it obtains the credit which it deserves with us by the testimony of the Spirit. For though it conciliate our reverence by its internal majesty, it never seriously affects till it is confirmed by the Spirit in our hearts'.[2]

'Let us bless God, then, for his inspired Word!' says Dr Warfield. 'And may He grant that we may always cherish, love, and venerate it, and conform all our life and thinking to it! So may we find safety for our feet, and peaceful security for our souls'.[3]

[1] *The Bible Tells Us So*, Banner of Truth Trust, 1968, p. 24.
[2] Book 1, James Clarke & Co Ltd, 1935, pp. 79, 80.
[3] *Revelation and Inspiration*, Oxford University Press, 1927, p. 425.

Other Booklets in this series:

Biblical Church Discipline, *Daniel Wray*

The Carnal Christian, *E. C. Reisinger*

Christians Grieve Too, *D. Howard*

Coming to Faith in Christ, *John Benton*

The Cross – The Vindication of God, *D. M. Lloyd-Jones*

The Five Points of Calvinism, *W. J. Seaton*

The Importance of The Local Church, *D. Wray*

The Invitation System, *Iain H. Murray*

The Moral Basis of Faith, *Tom Wells*

Open your Mouth for the Dumb, *Peter Barnes*

Origins?, *B. G. Ranganathan*

The Practical Implications of Calvinism, *A. N. Martin*

Reading the Bible, *Geoffrey Thomas*

Victory: The Work of the Spirit, *P. Potgieter*

What is a Biblical Christian?, *A. N. Martin*

What is the Reformed Faith?, *J. R. de Witt*

*Write for free 40pp illustrated Catalogue to:*

THE BANNER OF TRUTH TRUST
*3 Murrayfield Road, Edinburgh EH12 6EL*
*P.O. Box 621, Carlisle, Pennsylvania, 17013, U.S.A.*